99 Silhouette Patterns

for the Scroll Saw

by Terence Calway

Fox
Chapel Publishing Co. Inc.

1970 Broad Street • East Petersburg, PA 17520 • www.foxchapelpublishing.com

99 *Silhouette Patterns for the Scroll Saw* is a brand new work, first published in 2002 by Fox Chapel Publishing Company, Inc. The patterns contained herein are copyrighted by the author. Artists purchasing this book have permission to make up to 200 cutouts of each individual pattern. Persons or companies wishing to make more than 200 cutouts must notify the author for permission. The patterns themselves, however, are not to be duplicated for resale or distribution under any circumstances.

Publisher	Alan Giagnocavo
Book Editor	Ayleen Stellhorn
Desktop Specialist	Linda L. Eberly, Eberly Designs Inc.
Cover Design	Tim Mize

Additional cover artwork scrolled by Barry Gross (red Corian™ rooster, blue Corian™ hummingbird), Tim Schofield (fox napkin holders, horse napkin holders) and Joan West (butterfly candle holder, brass dragonfly and plastic dragonfly).

ISBN 1–56523–176–7
Library of Congress Preassigned Card Number 2001098359

To order your copy of this book,
please send check or money order
for the cover price plus $3.00 shipping to:
Fox Books
1970 Broad Street
East Petersburg, PA 17520

Or visit us on the web at
www.foxchapelpublishing.com

Manufactured in the USA

Table of Contents

About the Author

Terence Calway is a master electrician at a manufacturing facility. He enjoys bowling and playing hockey. He is an avid woodworker who enjoys scroll sawing and pattern designing in his spare time. He currently lives just outside Buffalo, New York, with his wife and daughter. This is his first book for Fox Chapel Publishing.

Basic Cutting Instructions

Silhouette patterns are an easy, yet elegant way to make creative scrolled designs. All of the patterns in this book are drawn in a similar format. I find this horseshoe shape ideal for displaying the finished silhouettes. You can use the patterns as is for table art, napkin holders, window hangers, nightlights and many other practical and decorative items. Just add a little imagination.

How to Begin

Start by trimming ⅛-inch or ¼-inch plywood or luan to 6-inch by 6-inch pieces. I usually cut a whole sheet of plywood or luan at one time. This way, all my "blanks" are cut and ready to go.

Next, glue the pattern to one of the blanks, making sure that the grain is running top to bottom. (See Photo 1.) I use rubber cement to attach my patterns.

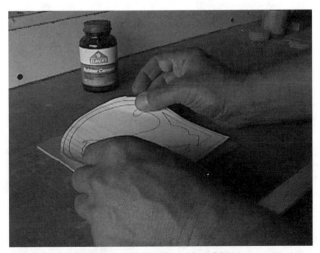

1. Glue the pattern to the base with rubber cement.

2. Hold multiple blanks together with finishing nails.

3. Drill starter holes in the inside cutout areas.

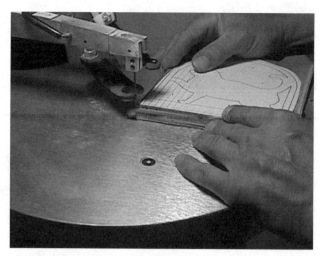

4. Cut the outside pattern line first.

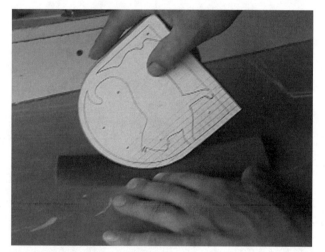

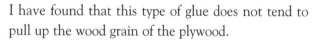

5. Sand the outside edges smooth.

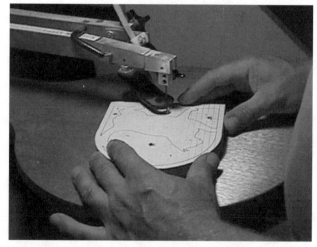

6. Cut the smallest inside cuts; then the larger inside cuts.

I have found that this type of glue does not tend to pull up the wood grain of the plywood.

To stack-cut the silhouette and make more than one copy at a time, place four or five blanks under the blank with the glued-up pattern. Make sure that all the wood grain is running top to bottom.

Carefully drive brads or finishing nails into the cutout areas of the stack. (See Photo 2.) Do not place the nails too close to the pattern lines. The back piece of plywood has a tendency to splinter as the nails are driven through. I try to keep the thickness of the whole stack under one inch high. This will keep the wood from burning and the blade from breaking during the cutting process.

After securing the blanks together, drill a hole in each inside cut. (See Photo 3.) This will be the hole

through which your saw blade will fit. Again, try not to drill the holes too close to the pattern edges; the wood on the back side of the stack may splinter. A ¼-inch drill bit works well for larger areas; try a ½₂-inch drill bit in smaller areas.

Ready to Cut

After you have mounted the pattern, stacked the blanks securely, and drilled the holes, you are ready to start cutting the silhouettes. I start by using a #9 or #12 blade with reverse teeth to cut the outside line of the pattern. (See Photo 4.) I have found that the reverse tooth blade prevents the bottom piece of plywood from splintering beyond repair.

Next, make the inside cuts. Choose a blade that you feel comfortable using. I usually use a #5 reverse

7. The stacked pieces come apart easily.

8. Use a router to round over the top edges of the base.

9. Use a router to make the slot for the silhouette.

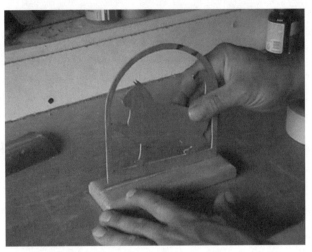

10. A couple drops of glue hold the silhouette in the base.

tooth blade to cut the larger openings and a #2 reverse tooth to cut out the finer lines in the pattern. Start with the smaller openings and work your way up to the larger openings. (See Photo 6.)

After you have cut the complete pattern, the pieces will free themselves easily. Remove the burrs and sand the edges smooth. Sand both sides of the silhouette so that both sides can be presented as finished surfaces.

Making the Base

To make the base as shown in Photo 10 you will need a router. A table saw is also helpful, but not nec-

essary. If you are not using a table saw, simply purchase pre-cut 1-inch by 3-inch wood of your choice.

If you are using a table saw, purchase 1-inch by 6-inch wood of your choice and rip it in half. Cut these 1-inch by 3-inch pieces into 6-inch lengths. Use a ⅜-inch roundover bit with a bearing guide to round over the top edge on all four sides. (See Photo 8.)

Finish all the wood you cut so you don't have to re-set the router for each piece. After the top edges are rounded over, cut the groove in the base to accept the silhouette. Use a straight bit that is the same diameter as the silhouette's thickness. Set the guide on the router to cut a slot in the center of the base ¼

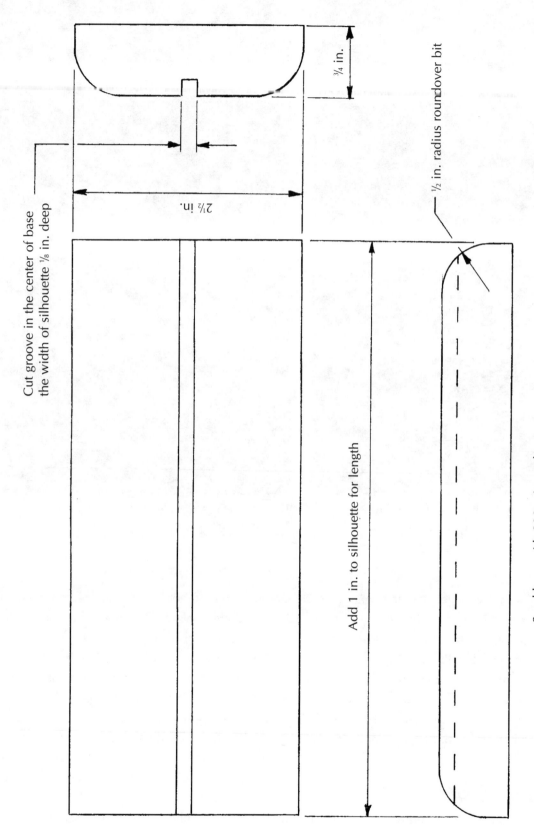

Cut groove in the center of base
the width of silhouette ⅛ in. deep

¾ in.

2½ in.

½ in. radius roundover bit

Add 1 in. to silhouette for length

Sand base with 220 grit sandpaper
Finish with stain or polyurethane

BASE

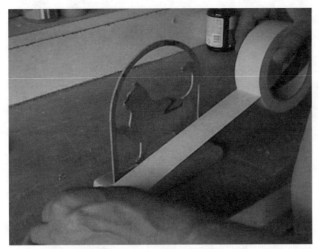

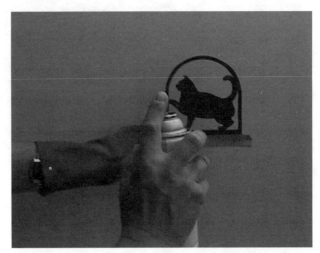

11. Use masking tape to protect the base from finishes and paint.

12. A final coat of finish is applied to the entire project.

to ⅜-inch deep. Finally, sand the base with 220 sandpaper.

Finishing and Assembly

Stain or paint the base to your liking. I have found that using a clear spray urethane finish seems to work well. I line up all the bases I have made, then spray two or three coats of clear urethane over all of the bases. Be sure to let the urethane dry to a hard finish. Caution: Be sure to use a well ventilated area when using spray finishes and paints.

Once the bases are dry, put the silhouette picture in the groove. Place two or three drops of wood glue in the slot. Then push the silhouette in, making sure it's centered and straight up and down. Let the piece dry for several hours.

Now it's time to paint the silhouette. Use masking tape to cover the base and protect it from the spray paint. Spray a coat of primer and a coat of flat black finish paint on the silhouette, making sure to get into all the nooks and crannies. After the paint dries, remove the masking tape from the base. Your silhouette project is now complete.

Variations

Many different projects can be made from these patterns. I have asked several artists who work in different mediums to create the artwork shown here.

Some tips for making these projects follow. Use your imagination to come up with other ideas.

Nightlights—Reduce the size of the pattern and cut the silhouette from colored plastic. Glue the finished plastic silhouette to a standard nightlight.

Trivets—Enlarge the size of the pattern and cut the silhouette from Corian or other solid surface materials. The finished trivet makes an ideal addition to any kitchen and will protect countertops and tabletops from hot pots and pans.

Lanterns—Cut four silhouettes and a square base, then glue them together at right angles to create a lantern for a votive candle. You may want to cut the silhouettes from thicker wood or even metal.

Napkin Holders—Cut two silhouettes and a rectangular base from thicker wood and glue the pieces together at right angles to create a decorative tabletop napkin holder.

Letter Holders—Construct a letter holder in the same manner as the napkin holder. Consider adding several silhouettes to make a separate space for outgoing letters and incoming letters.

Window Hangers—Fill in the spaces of a wood silhouette with liquid colors that harden to create a festive suncatcher. Reduce the size of the silhouette and add a magnet to the back to make refrigerator decorations that will hold notes and recipes.

1.
Screaming
Macaw

Copy at 125%

2.
Perched
Macaw

Copy at 125%

Copy at 125%

4.
Cat Bird

Copy at 125%

5.
Parrot

Copy at 125%

6.
Woodpecker

Copy at 125%

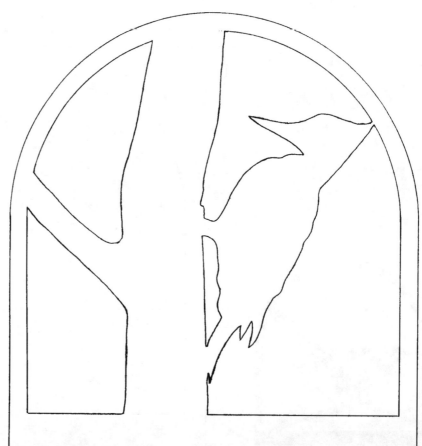

7.
Hummingbird
and Flower

Copy at 125%

8.
Hummingbird
in Flight

Copy at 125%

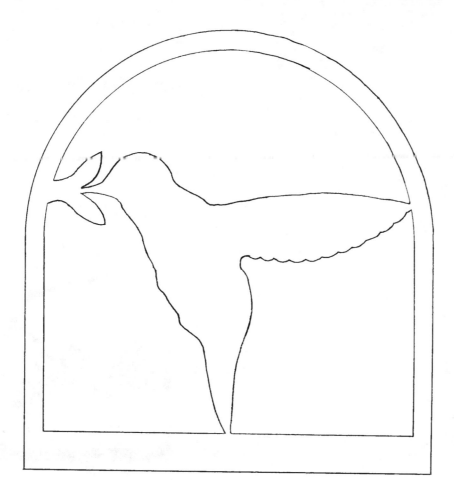

9.
Hovering
Hummingbird

Copy at 125%

10.
Duck in
Flight

Copy at 125%

11. Geese

Copy at 125%

12. Flamingo Pair

Copy at 125%

13.
Resting
Flamingo

Copy at 125%

14.
Hawk

Copy at 125%

15.
Ostrich

Copy at 125%

16.
Pelican

Copy at 125%

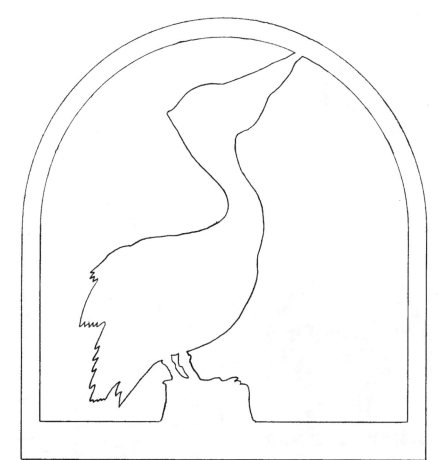

17.
Swan

Copy at 125%

18.
Cat

Copy at 125%

19.
House Cat

Copy at 125%

20.
Playful
Kittens

Copy at 125%

21.
Prowling
Cat

Copy at 125%

22.
Royal
Cat

Copy at 125%

23. Playful Cat

Copy at 125%

24. Cat and Butterfly

Copy at 125%

25.
Scared
Cat

Copy at 125%

26.
Attentive
Cat

Copy at 125%

27.
Cat and
Fish

Copy at 125%

28.
Cat
Pair

Copy at 125%

29.
Golden
Retriever

Copy at 125%

30.
Labrador
Retriever

Copy at 125%

32.
Boxer

Copy at 125%

34.
Begging Dog

Copy at 125%

35.
Collie

Copy at 125%

36.
Puppy

Copy at 125%

38.
Greyhound

Copy at 125%

39.
Leaping
Greyhound

Copy at 125%

40.
Monarch

Copy at 125%

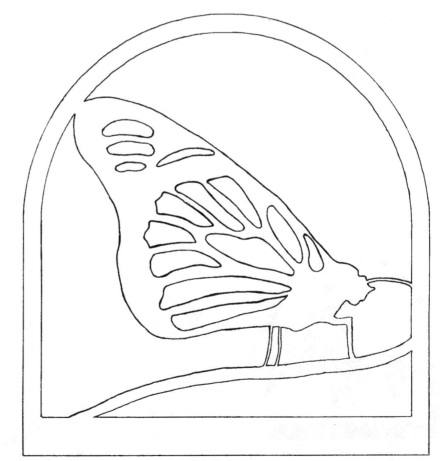

43.
Purplish
Copper

Copy at 125%

44.
Giant
Swallowtail

Copy at 125%

45.
Meadow
Fritillary

Copy at 125%

46.
American
Painted Lady

Copy at 125%

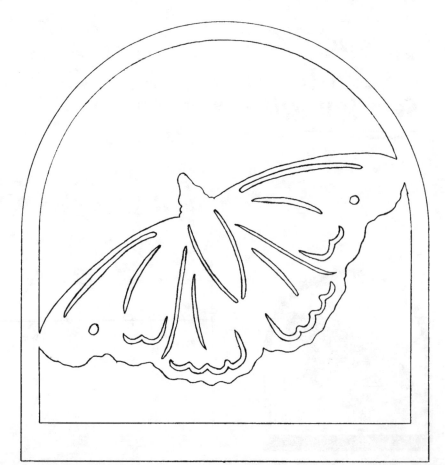

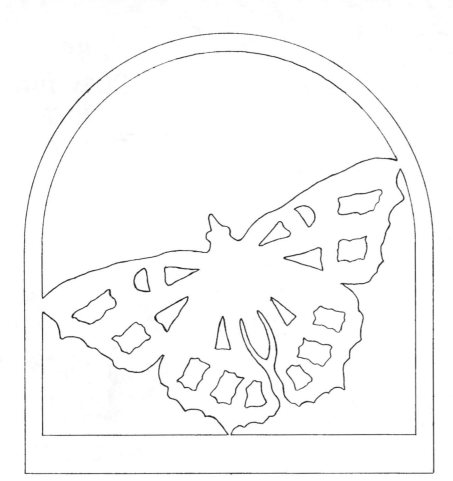

48.
Swallowtail

Copy at 125%

50.
Southern
Dog Face

Copy at 125%

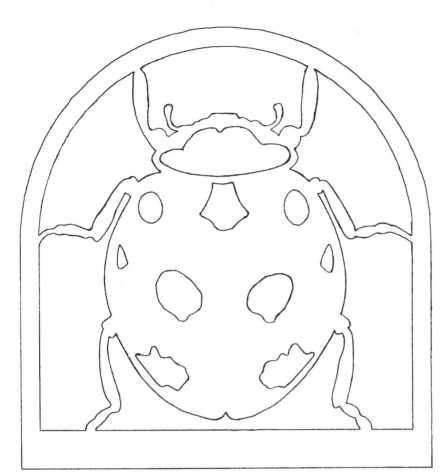

51.
Ladybug

Copy at 125%

52.
Dragonfly

Copy at 125%

99 Silhouette Patterns for the Scroll Saw

53.
Jumping
Horse

Copy at 125%

54.
English Horse
& Rider

Copy at 125%

55.
Bucking
Bronco

Copy at 125%

56.
Racing
Horse

Copy at 125%

57.
Wild
Mustang

Copy at 125%

58.
Chicken

Copy at 125%

59.
Rooster

Copy at 125%

60.
Bull

Copy at 125%

61.
Watchful
Rabbit

Copy at 125%

62.
Curious
Rabbit

Copy at 125%

63.
Balancing
Squirrel

Copy at 125%

64.
Squirrel
and Nut

Copy at 125%

65.
Ferret

Copy at 125%

66.
Ferret

Copy at 125%

67.
Skunk

Copy at 125%

68.
Fox

Copy at 125%

69.
Woodland
Buck

Copy at 125%

70.
Eight-Point
Buck

Copy at 125%

71.
Moose

Copy at 125%

72.
Buffalo

Copy at 125%

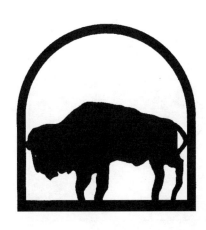

74.
Lion

Copy at 125%

75.
Tiger

Copy at 125%

76.
Panther

Copy at 125%

77.
Rhinoceros

Copy at 125%

78.
Elephant

Copy at 125%

79.
Bull
Elephant

Copy at 125%

80.
Trumpeting
Elephant

Copy at 125%

81.
Monkey

Copy at 125%

82.
Baboon

Copy at 125%

83.
Camel

Copy at 125%

84.
Owl

Copy at 125%

85.
Kangaroo

Copy at 125%

86.
Bounding
Kangaroo

Copy at 125%

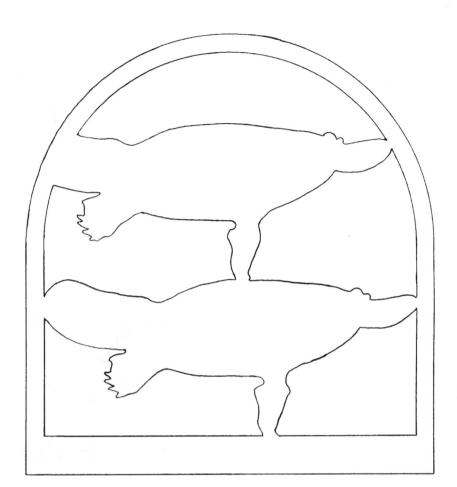

87.
Platypus

Copy at 125%

88.
Alligator

Copy at 125%

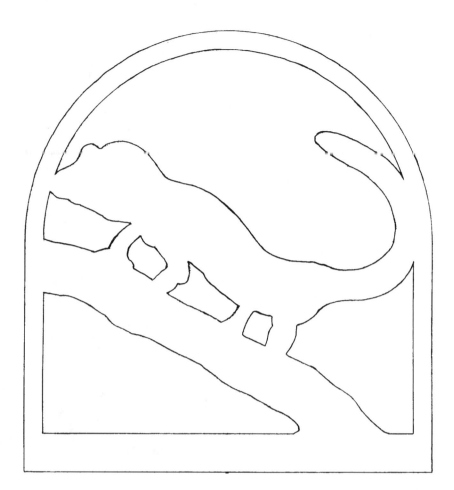

89.
Gecko

Copy at 125%

90.
Box
Turtle

Copy at 125%

91.
Pond
Turtle

Copy at 125%

92.
Frog

Copy at 125%

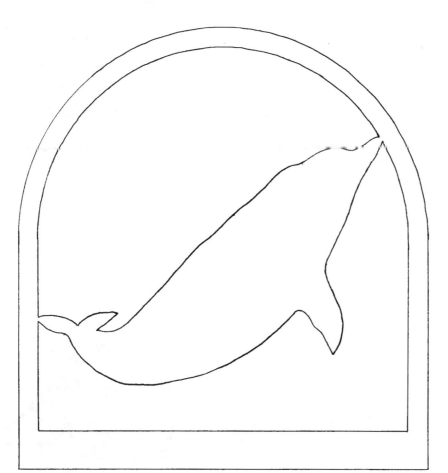

93.
Swimming Dolphin

Copy at 125%

94.
Leaping Dolphin

Copy at 125%

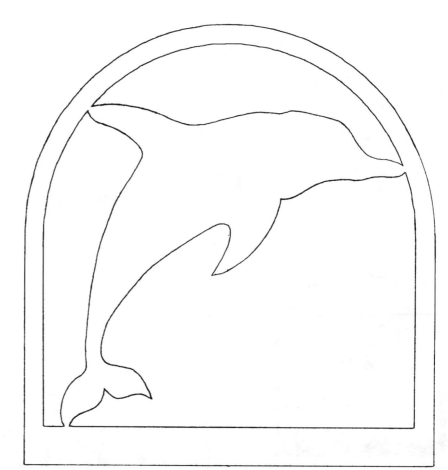

95.
Orca

Copy at 125%

96.
Lobster

Copy at 125%

97.
Seahorse

Copy at 125%

98.
Fish Pair

Copy at 125%

Copy at 125%

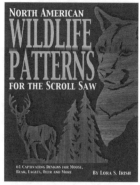
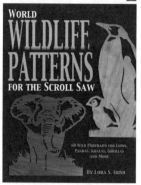
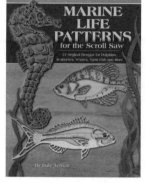